Dance With Me

by Barbara Juster Esbensen

illustrated by Megan Lloyd

HarperCollins*Publishers*

This book is dedicated to everyone who likes
the dance and the swing of a rhyme now and then
—BJE

For Tom, in celebration of our moose dance
—ML

Dance With Me
Text copyright © 1995 by Barbara Juster Esbensen
Illustrations copyright © 1995 by Megan Lloyd

Library of Congress Cataloging-in-Publication Data
Esbensen, Barbara Juster.
    Dance with me / by Barbara Juster Esbensen ; illustrated by Megan Lloyd.
        p.   cm.
    Summary: A collection of poems depicting the dance of nature.
    ISBN 0-06-022793-1. — ISBN 0-06-022823-7 (lib. bdg.)
    1. Dancing—Juvenile poetry.   2. Dancers—Juvenile poetry.   3. Children's poetry,
American.   [1. Nature—Poetry.   2. Dancing—Poetry.   3. American poetry.]
I. Lloyd, Megan, ill.   II. Title.
PS3555.S24D36   1995   93-48442
811'.54—dc20   CIP
                                                                                   AC

Typography by Al Cetta   1 2 3 4 5 6 7 8 9 10   ❖   First Edition

The illustrations in this book were prepared using
Conté crayons and soft pastels on Sabretooth pastel paper.

Poems

Invitation to the Wind

Dance
with me
now
in the Springlight
dance
with me under the sky.
Dance
on
your
tiptoes and turn me and
whirl me and lift me
and teach me to fly!
Carry me
on your wild shoulders
I'll
catch all the petals
that spill!
Dance with me,
Wind,
like
you
dance
with the kites
Like you dance with those kites
on the hill!

The Wind's Reply
For B. F.

Yes,
thank you
for asking   Just
give me your hand
As soon as I've
showered I'm yours to
command

I'll wear my bright
banners   my coat
with the leaves
embroidered in emerald on
April-blue sleeves

We'll fly to the morning
where everything's
new
I'm shining my
dancing shoes
child
just for you

Gardener

Bend
straighten
fast
slow
she's
teaching
a stiff little dance
to the hoe
Back
forth
push
pull
the
bucket of weeds
is nearly full
Earth
hums
bees
know
zinnias
daisies
pansies
grow
to the sunlit rhythm
of Mother's hoe

Bubbles

Just air
blown there
made round
and hollow
and fragile
and thin
with rainbow skin
and more to follow
to float
in the sky
to go dancing by

A dance of breath
that has learned
to fly!

Lightning Dance

En garde! Touché!
A dance of blades
Swordplay!
Parry! Thrust!   Fall back!
This is all-out
attack!

Thunder bangs
its drum
from all sides
come
dagger dirk and scimitar
slicing up the
farthest star

Excalibur
blazes
light—
King Arthur rides the storm
tonight!

Mirror Dancer

We
cannot hear the music
We
cannot tap the beat
The
baby in the mirror
laughs
and
stamps
her silent feet

My baby sister
copies her
They spread
their fingers wide
She touches noses
with the glass
and tries to dance
inside!

The Grandparent Glide

The music   Big Band
She flashes
a glance   She
holds out her hand
and
they dance

Her light hand
on his shoulder
his arm
round her waist
They stop growing older
their fingers tight-laced

Slowly their toes
print a dance
on the rug
and everyone knows
when he gives her a hug

How can they tell
when to stop   when
to start?
—I know him so well!
—I know her by heart!

Performance

In moonlit pantomime
the trees
lock crooked arms
and step across the lawn

Up from the river flats
a breeze
remembers how to rhyme
its whispered song

And from our drowsy beds
we seize
the liquid melody
and hum along

Basketball Ballet

How
easy
to score
if you
float
off
the
floor

The ball
in the
cup
of your
hand
pulls you

up

A soft plunk!
a slam dunk
and light
as a thistle
you land

It's a
sure thing
to score
if you
know how
to float
off
the
floor!

Flower-Ballerinas

Suspended
from a fragile
strand
they're set in motion
by the breeze

Beneath
this puppet master's
hand
they dance in ruffled
twos and threes

These ballerinas
lightly
pose
with every arm
a petaled arc

They twirl and
turn on pointed
toes
each jeweled shoe
a fuchsia spark

Danceline at High Tide

Watch with me here
    on the gravelly beach
     The afternoon show
is about to begin

Watch how the waves
    in their snow-flower capes
     bend at the waist
and come tumbling in

How each spangled knee joint
    kicks out a green stocking
     How rows of green water legs
kneel on the sand

The quicksilver rocking
       of trailing blue petticoats
       flashing with minnowtails
covers your hand

Do you see how they bow
       to their onrushing partners
       obeying the moon
and the wind's tomtom beat?

When the moon and the wind
       tell the dancers to exit
       they curtsy a lacy good-bye
at your feet

Roof Dancers

With
a tappity-tap on
the roof in
the rain   they dance
in my dream with
top hat and cane

With a tappity toe
and a clickety heel
they
timestep and
flatstep
and hopstep and wheel

They bow to the footlights!
They wave to the drummer!
My
tap-dancing
high-stepping
hoofers of summer

Mirage

Ahead of the car
the pavement
shimmers
in windless
summer air
where
wavery dancers glimmer
and lift
their drift-
ing watery
hair

They sway above
the pavement   they
slide on invisible feet
and
move in a colorless
ghostly
dance
under summer sun
and heat

Shadow Dancers

Sun shadow
tree shadow
holding-hands-with-me
shadow

Shadow stand
shadow
bend
I'm dancing with my
shadow friend
Two shadows flit
along the wall
Two shadows
leap
Two shadows
fall

Race with me
shadow
in the sun
Run
my shadow
Run! Run! Run!

Dust Dancers

Twinkling
and small
as the point of a pin
the dust dancers all
wait to float in

They wait
in the gloom
for a sunspike of light
to stab through the room
and illumine their flight

If you breathe
on the crowd
their rhythms are stirred
and you're only allowed
the tiniest word

Clouds
make them hide
but they shine in the sun
and as hard as I've tried
I have never caught one!